THE CASE OF NORA

BOOKS BY MOSHE FELDENKRAIS

Awareness Through Movement

Awareness Through Movement (illustrated)

Adventures in the Jungle of the Brain
The Case of Nora: *Body Awareness as Healing Therapy*

The Case of Nora

BODY AWARENESS AS HEALING THERAPY

MOSHE FELDENKRAIS

1817

HARPER & ROW, PUBLISHERS

NEW YORK, HAGERSTOWN, SAN FRANCISCO

LONDON

FIRST EDITION

Designed by Sidney Feinberg

Library of Congress Cataloging in Publication Data

Feldenkrais, Moshé, 1904–
   The case of Nora.
   (His Adventures in the jungle of the brain)
   1. Brain damage. 2. Brain—localization of functions. 3. Mind and body. 4. Higher nervous activity. I. Title. II. Series: Feldenkrais, Moshé, 1904–   Adventures in the jungle of the brain.
RC386.2.F44 1977   616.8'1'09   76–62935
ISBN 0–06–062346–2

---

77 78 79 80 81 10 9 8 7 6 5 4 3 2 1

Contents

Preface   5

Introduction   7

1. Who Is Nora?   11

2. A Way Out of the Maze   19

3. Mistakes: Part of Learning   35

4. Improving vs. Curing   47

5. Talking without Words   52

6. Sensing to Understand   67

THE ESSENCE   77

QUESTIONS—AND AVOIDING
ANSWERING THEM FULLY   87

Preface

The case of Nora is the first of a series of stories out of my practice. Each one describes a part of my work with people.

I use two techniques. One is nonverbal manipulation of an individual and is called Functional Integration. The other, used in large groups of all ages, is verbal and is called Awareness Through Movement.

Both techniques enlarge awareness of self and thereby lead to a better lifestyle. They teach methodical ways of using our faculties that many of us stumble into by chance. It is these faculties that make us tick.

This true story was actually told to an audience. The working theory is somewhere between intuition and future scientific gospel.

Introduction

There are many kinds and ways of learning. Some illiterate men have learned more and better than you and I.

There is the learning of a skill; there is the kind of learning in which we enlarge our knowledge or understanding of what we already know. And there is the most important kind of learning which goes with physical growth. By this last I mean learning in which quantity grows and changes to a new quality, and not the mere accumulation of knowledge, useful as this may be. Often we do not see this kind of learning at all; it can go on for more or less lengthy periods of time, apparently aimlessly, and then a new form of action appears as if from nowhere.

Most truly important things are learned in this way. There was no method, no system in our learning to walk, speak, or count, no examinations, no prescribed term in which to complete the learning, no preset, clearly expressed aim to be attained. This apparently aimless method produces practically no failures of learning in the normally constituted human, and under its conditions we become mature persons, whether well educated or completely illiterate. Formal teachings from childhood to adulthood seems to overlook the fact that there are ways of learning that lead to growth and maturity with practically no failures. Formal teaching is more concerned with "what" is taught than with "how"; its failures are very frequent.

There are teachers in this world without whom it would be even less cheerful than it is. The drawback is that there are so few of them; one can more easily win a lottery than have one of them as a mentor.

The present case illustrates a method in which the learning of the pupil, and not teaching, is the essence. Suppose I teach you a theorem in geometry; I expose the theorem, try to reason with you, then repeat what I said several times until you seem able to do so too. This is the kind of teaching that goes on until you can say or even understand the matter as I do. Where learning and physical growth are concerned, the teaching I have just described is to my mind futile. To produce learning in you I have to devise a method which will cause you to think the theorem as another man did before you. As a teacher I can accelerate your learning by presenting the experience under the conditions in which the human brain learned in the first place. Such teaching requires more than the ability to teach theory at the blackboard.

The story I will tell you recreates the situation which lead to learning, and I will then develop the theory. I hope you will, in fact, discern the theory before I explain it. At the end of the discussion of theory I will answer your questions.

THE CASE OF NORA

1

Who Is Nora?

Some three years ago I was visiting Switzerland. I had become quite well known there through my radio broadcasts and many people had written to me, including a woman who asked me to see her sister, Nora, a well-educated and intelligent woman in her sixties who held an important position and spoke several languages. One morning Nora had found that she had difficulty in getting out of bed; her body was somewhat stiff and her speech a bit slow and rather slurred. She had no alternative but to stay in bed.

The local doctor's diagnosis was that she probably had had a clot or some sort of hemorrhage. After a few days, feeling a little better, Nora got up but found her speech impaired; she could speak clearly but rather slowly. Later, when she tried to read the morning paper, everything suddenly became a blur and she realized that she could neither read nor write. She became panicky and was taken to a neurological clinic in Zurich where it was established that there was some injury to the left side of the brain. Since it was circulatory damage only, it was hoped that it would improve unaided. Nora was not paralyzed but only slightly spastic on one side more than the other. With time, her speech improved but not her reading nor her writing. She could no longer write her own name, nor read it written or printed. She would hold a pencil in her hand more like a tool, and even when she held the pencil properly, she could do no more than scribble on the paper.

After nearly a year, when neither writing nor reading improved, Nora was taken home.

But then, even in her own home she had some trouble in finding her way. She could not locate doors and she often bumped into furniture. In spite of all this, her intelligence was almost unimpaired. When spoken to, her eyes looked as if it were difficult for her to understand but, in fact, she understood everything and answered to the point. When sitting on a chair and talking, she would speak and answer almost normally and look unremarkable to a stranger. However, she suffered from deep depression and sometimes spent hours on end saying and doing nothing. She slept very well and would also fall asleep during the day. She was given drugs intended to reduce the clotting of the blood and to avoid another mishap. However, feeling that the drugs were not helping her very much, she refused at times to take them. When her sister insisted, she had no alternative but to keep on taking them. As a result, she was constantly depressed and had very little will of her own. She needed attention day and night. When I first saw Nora, I did not think that it was a very hopeful case. But, as I was her relatives' last hope, I put her on a table and began to examine the movements of her head.

Maybe it has not occurred to you that the head—quite apart from its contents—is a very important thing; it carries all the teleceptors, and so, the way we perform an action connected with our senses affects the way we move the head. It may be stiff so that, to turn it, one has to turn one's body also. An injured neck, spine, or muscle will also affect the movements of the head. One can feel it when trying to move another's head with one's hands: the head movements may be jerky, not continually smooth, regular, or even all around. One may be able to turn the head with both hands ten degrees and no further; then if one turns the head back to the middle position a few times, one finds that it will move a few more degrees. This means that when the person is upright the motion of the head around the horizon is also irregular, stiff, sticky, or limited in extent. The eyes move with the head but can also move relative to it, so much so that the faulty movement may be attributed originally to the eyes.

Examination of the movement of the head gives a fair idea of the state of the use of self and an idea of the consciousness and awareness of the body examined. This examination serves at the same time as an improvement or reminder to improve the movement of the head; examination and treatment are practically the same.

Examining Nora's head, and gradually reducing the intensity of my touch and of movements for finer appreciation, had an effect on the muscles of her neck, and her head became easier and smoother to move. I felt that she responded very well; her face became alive, her eyes brightened, and her depression disappeared gradually.

As I examined her legs, arms, body and chest for the quality of the movement—not just how much but first of all how easily they could be moved—she relaxed further. I pushed the sole of one foot and watched carefully to determine whether I could make her legs push the pelvis and, through the spine, affect her head. This is easy only when the muscles and skeleton are normal. If the muscles relax and have their normal tonus, not too much and not too little, the head tilts in a way which indicates whether the skeleton transmits the push in the foot properly. (What is proper or improper will be explained later.) After I examined the cardinal movements of her body for about three-quarters of an hour, Nora became quite cheerful and looked much brighter. Her sister and other relatives in the room observed that the expression of her face and eyes and her facial mobility changed almost to normal.

I then seated her at a table, put a pencil in her hand, and with her hand in mine, wrote the figures 3, 4, 7, and 9. I guided the hand which held the pencil and she could read the figures after writing them. I moved her hand and wrote the figures again and then asked her what she was writing. She said "34." Her relatives looked as if they could not believe that she could have so improved in one lesson that she was able to write figures and recognize them. They said that nothing like this had been achieved during her previous treatments.

I knew, of course, that very often such patients can read figures much easier than letters, depending on the location of the injury. Professor Paul Broca, who was one of the first to examine war cases with head injuries and the initiator of the neurological research which led to better understanding of the functioning of the brain, found that some head-injured soldiers could see the phrase, "the 27th of July" and fail to know the meaning yet had no difficulty with the figures "27/7." I knew this difference between reading letters and figures and I took a chance. I decided not to try her reading anything other than figures so as to avoid her discouragement through possible failure.

After a rest, I tried again. This time I seated Nora on a chair and tried to examine and improve the movement of her eyes and head. I wanted to see whether I could, by gently guiding her head, bring her from the chair to a standing position in a smooth and continuous way. At the start, she was stiff, especially on the right side, and I could not bend her elbow, her hand, or leg; the members felt unyielding and stiff like a poker, as is the case with spastics. I proceeded very slowly and gently to work on the articulations. She yielded rather nicely; the head motion became soft and the shoulders loose, but still far from normal. However, it had improved from the initial state to such a degree that she could feel the change.

At the beginning I moved the head with my hands so that the eyes were directed a bit downward, and then pulled the head gently, following the direction of the cervical spine, which is the normal movement of the head and the eyes when getting up. A person in a healthy state gets up when his head is so manipulated; without being told, he feels the clue and acts upon it. But Nora felt heavy to my hands and like a pillar. She did not understand the hint given by my hands to her head. Trying again and again, and softening my grip and movement, I succeeded in lifting her with relatively small effort to the standing position, and then in making her sit again. She soon learned to recognize the pressure imparted to the head as a signal for standing and then sitting down again.

The onlookers were moved and someone remarked that if it worked like that she would be cured in no time. For my part I thought that it might take a year or more of daily lessons. I believed that it might come out well, but, being not at all sure, I told them that I did not think it was worthwhile to send Nora to me in Israel. She would have to fly there, quite an expensive proposition in itself, and since she would be in a foreign country, without knowing the language, someone would have to accompany her and stay with her. What would they do with themselves? I could give her lessons for half an hour daily, as I do usually, but for the rest of the time somebody would have to keep an eye on her until she might improve sufficiently to be on her own. There was also the question of whether I would succeed.

Next morning, however, I received a telephone call from her family. After deliberation they had decided that to take Nora to Israel would not significantly increase the cost of her care. It took two persons to keep her at home, one during the day and the other during the night, which in itself was very expensive. She had to be watched constantly. When she got up during the night she could not find the door; often she banged her head and then got panicky on not finding her way back to bed. During the day she tried to go out and then could not find her way back, or did not know where she had intended to go. At home she was a constant worry to them. Always afraid that something might happen to her, her family kept telephoning and asking how she was. They also held the conviction that at home Nora could only get worse. If she went to Israel there was a possibility that she would improve. As she had some savings and a pension, they had decided that she should go to Israel and her siblings would share the burden. They preferred giving her a chance to electing the certainty of slow extinction.

I decided to continue my examination before finally accepting the responsibility. I had to make it clear to them that I was not promising a cure but only that I would do my best. I would not have accepted at all if I had no hope that the enterprise might be worthwhile in the end.

During the subsequent examination I asked Nora to lie on a couch. She had considerable difficulty; she fumbled, turned, and could not make up her mind. I had asked her to lie on her back with her head nearest me, so I made this request again word by word. It was obvious that she had heard me but she either did not understand or was not able to produce the movement readily. I asked her family whether they knew of this trouble and learned that her normal way of going to bed on her own initiative was uneventful. Now I could see that I was dealing with an asymmetrical functioning of the two hemispheres of the brain. It will be easier for you to follow me if you understand something of the history of brain research.

In the last century Professor Broca, whose name I have mentioned, noticed in treating soldiers with head injuries that a bullet or a bit of shrapnel lodged in the right hemisphere caused paralysis of the left side of the body. An equal injury to the left hemisphere was accompanied by another loss of function, namely speech. It soon became clear that in right-handed people the speech is controlled by the left hemisphere and therefore injury to the left side of the head generally produced not only paralysis of the right arm and leg, but also aphasia or loss of speech. As the number of true left-handed people constitutes only a small percentage of the population, it was rare that injury to the right hemisphere could lead to loss of speech. The soldiers who had paralysis with loss of speech following extraction of bullets or shrapnel from the right side of the head were true left-handed people.

The two hemispheres of the brain are not equivalent, let alone identical. This asymmetry has been intuitively suspected by many. The Russian physiologist, Ivan Pavlov, believed that humans are essentially either thinkers or artists. Igor Markevitch, the famous conductor, once told me that he firmly believed that the left ear hears melody, and the right is more analytic of the structures of music and can tell one note from another. Today the accumulated studies of Wilder Penfield and the more recent work of Roger Sperry on epileptics have made it generally accepted knowledge that the right hemisphere controls functions such as the imaginative, nonverbal memory and concrete thinking, while the left controls speech, writing, and abstract thinking.

I will return to the subject when we reach the treatment stage of Nora's case. You will appreciate more fully the beauty of what was done when you know some details of the relationship of function and structure in the working of the brain. For now it is sufficient to note that this relationship lay at the core of Nora's difficulty, and that I agreed, finally, to treat her, to her family's relief.

2

A Way Out of the Maze

I returned to Israel. In anticipation of Nora's arrival, I did a lot of thinking as I do with each pupil, or patient. I have no stereotyped technique to apply ready-made to everyone; this is against the principles of my theory. I search and, if possible, find a major difficulty which can be detected at each session and which may, if worked upon, soften and be partially removed. I daily change the position or situation of the patient. As you may have guessed from my initial examinations, I do not repeat mechanically one day the manipulations of the day before, but go slowly and progressively through every function of the body. Structure and function are tied so intimately that one cannot easily separate them nor deal with one without involving the other. In the light of the earlier experience with Nora, I worked out my program in very general terms. I also prepared myself to change my outlook with subsequent examinations of the affected functions and to let these findings guide me in my judgment and my daily conduct of the case.

From the start I expected to find more defects than just the one discovered in my preliminary examinations. No two patients are affected equally. It is, however, rather unusual that a patient is apparently only slightly affected bodily and appears normal in her intelligence, yet is so badly affected in writing and reading. I believed, on the basis of difficulties such as not finding her way at night and bumping into furniture, that some other fundamental functions would prove to have been affected.

When Nora was brought to see me, I set out to find, in minute detail, what other abilities were impeded. She preferred to speak German, her mother tongue, so though my German is not very good, I too spoke German. When I asked her to lie on the couch on her back, she again began the series of maneuvers which I had observed when I examined her at her house.

At the time of this case I was engaged in teaching a group of my assistants. Every interesting case which could give them insight into my method was presented fully to them; thus Nora's treatment, which was to last several months, would often be given in the presence of my seminar. It should be understood that I never impose on a pupil the presence of even a visiting professor without obtaining the pupil's consent. For my seminar I accepted patients who agreed to the presence of onlookers and were relieved from paying any honorarium. But even with free patients I have private sessions too. Often a patient, when relieved from anxiety and muscular stiffness, will spontaneously recall and say things about himself which he would never do in the presence of others. It is therefore my custom to have a number of private lessons even when there is no objection to visitors.

My assistants observed Nora fumbling at lying on her back,

trying to put one knee on the couch and then the other, and finally not succeeding. They believed that she was shy and therefore self-conscious and awkward, since shyness can aggravate the inability to respond to a verbal concept and since she experienced no difficulty in doing the same act of her own accord. In the end, after having removed her shoes, I had to help her to lie on her back. As I was removing her shoes I suddenly realized that I should show my assistants very clearly that it was not a case of shyness but of sickness. My assistants seemed to believe that I was overtheorizing.

Very often at the end of a session I will assume the effort of bringing the patient from the position in which we worked to the standing position. For instance, I will assist a patient with considerable skeletal defects or muscular injuries to the standing position and make sure that he remains inactive and passive until the pressure on his feet mobilizes the reflexive act of standing.

One reason I do this is so that the change of organization and of the muscular tonus alteration accomplished in the treatment will not be lost by the patient's initial effort to get up, which he cannot but do in his habitual way. If the lesson is really good, he might even feel pain by using his habitual mode of action in a now changed body. Also, I want the patient to realize the often striking difference in sensation obtained in the standing position. Because this difference is produced bit by bit during treatment, it often escapes the awareness of the pupil. The accumulated result is sensed as an increase in height, erectness, floating lightness, and the like.

You will understand then why, at the end of the Session with Nora, I put my forearm behind her neck and my hand

on the shoulder blade farthest from me. I then bent her
knees, slid my other forearm over the top of her knees and
under both of them so that this hand was nearest to me. In
this situation it is very easy to swivel the person on the but-
tocks. Indeed, with the upper part of the body and the legs
in the air and the body bent, it feels like turning a wheel on
its axis. My female assistants can lift the heaviest patients to
the sitting position with ease and without holding their
breath.

I asked Nora to put on her shoes and I pushed her shoes
nearer to her feet. Without betraying my intention, I placed
the shoes so that the heels were farthest away from her feet.
She looked at me with an inquiring expression and tried to
push her feet into the shoes as they stood on the floor and of
course she could not. She was also unable to fit her shoes
correctly, that is, to put her left foot into the left shoe and the
right foot into the right shoes. She just could not find which
way which shoe went on which foot. After she fumbled for
five or six minutes, I helped her put them on. Her anxiety
being of no therapeutic value, I cut it short so as not to
increase her embarrassment before the assistants. Here was
a handsome lady with an intelligent sparkle in her eyes,
obviously a dominant yet benevolent person, unable to put
on her shoes.

Most people would be astonished, upon watching Nora
trying to put on her shoes, at the number of ways there are
to be wrong. It may be worth your while to try the many
other impossible arrangements and see how difficult it is to
slide the feet in by chance. Orientation in space and in time
gives direction and adroitness to whatever we do. It is useful

to experience the value of purposeful orientation as compared with succeeding by chance.

Later I realized more fully the extent of disruption of Nora's body awareness and orientation. Her relatives at home could not realize the extent of her trauma—both they and her nurses were used to putting on her shoes for her, since it was difficult for her to do so herself. After all, she was ill and needed help.

Here I found that my entire program required rethinking. I could see now that even sitting on a chair was not an action she performed directly or by design. Instead, she would try to sit on the side of the chair, not squarely and directly, but trying to fit herself to the chair obliquely, hoping that by dint of proximity her bottom would fit the chair.

My insistence on details of Nora's way of doing things will enable you to perceive how marvelous and elaborate is the way in which we normally function. How much of its beauty, utility, complexity, and simplicity we owe to learning! The fun of reading detective stories is not the plot, which we usually forget, but our conscious or unconscious curiosity about the solution, who really did it and *how*. The case of Nora is such a detective story which could not be solved without the details.

Because I was teaching I tried to impress on my students the necessity of evaluating trauma: to what age did the functions under examination regress? Guessing the age to which the patient has regressed is essential for planning the means for subsequent recovery. Growing means order. This natural order cannot be reversed or even neglected. We cannot teach a child to skate before he can walk. The order is fixed and we have to obey or fail. We are so used to certain phenomena that the order of their growth seems natural and we do not stop to think that it is also a necessity. We know now that Nora's orientation in space was faulty. But how can one correct such a deficiency, starting with what and doing what?

At the end of the session in which the incident of the shoes occurred, I told Nora that she might now go home. There were three doors in the room: one was locked permanently by a bar visible through the glass panels; one led to another room; through the third my patient had entered from the hall. This door had a frosted glass panel almost as big as the door itself through which the light in the hall could be seen. Nonetheless, Nora directed herself to the door leading to the next room and not to the door to the hall. When she found a strange room she tried the correct exit door. She groped with her right hand along the side with no handle; then she found the handle on her left, opened the door with her left hand and banged it against her head. She closed the door confused, red in the face, and exclaimed, "I cannot!" She was obviously ashamed of herself. As I have already told you, she was intelligent and her conversation could leave no doubt about her mental capacity. The difficulty was orientation in space, suddenly seen in relation to her right and left.

Orientation in space is an abstract notion and cannot be handled as such. I do not know how to improve on the words or the function "orientation in space" but I know how to help a person in distinguishing between right and left, in bettering his dexterity and precision of turning, so that when he performs his movements efficiently and precisely he has, in fact, improved his orientation in space.

You may be thinking that orientation in space is not more abstract than body awareness and that there is not much to choose between them. Body awareness is a more concrete concept consisting of our containing the kinesthetic sensation of the body, that is, the sensation of movement. Muscular-spatial-temporal sense contains orientation and is an important auxiliary to movement. Movement of a sane and healthy body is to help survival. The body of the person and his self—or his being—are inseparable. Yet the body—the material support of the self—is not the whole story. Awareness is learned. We have to learn that there is a sense of right and left which we carry with us. Nora's body awareness had failed her and she had regressed to an earlier state.

Have you ever asked yourself why a two-year-old child cannot put shoes on by himself? Or, at what age he should be able to do so? Does age have no meaning here besides the fact that many children can do it at a certain age and practically none who are younger? What actually happened in the preceding years that made it possible at a certain moment for one to put on one's shoes unaided? To help somebody to recover a lost function, one must answer these questions seriously and correctly.

Jean Piaget achieved world fame by establishing, among other things, the age at which we can do certain things. At what age can a child hop on his foot several times? At what age can a child appreciate what it is to be a quarter of an hour late? For instance, Piaget filled a glass with water, poured it into a long thin bottle, then refilled the same glass and poured it into a large short bottle. He found that before they are able to appreciate volume, children can evaluate length or extension and will invariably say that there is more water in the taller bottle. Only later will they connect the size of the glass with the volume of the bottles. This means that both learning and growth must take place before we can distinguish between shape and volume, otherwise shape is conceived as difference in length or size.

In a living being, movement means displacement in space external to the body, and also an enormous amount of internal nervous and muscular activity prior to the performance of such action. You probably know that areas of localization of simple or primitive movements on the motor cortex of the brain, when joined together, form a little figure of a man called *homunculus.* This little figure is not very obviously a human being. The size of its individual parts depends on the importance of the function performed by the part of the body it influences. The neural area representing the thumb is much larger than that of the thigh, the thumb being involved in almost every handling operation undertaken. The thigh, by contrast, rarely does more than move the knee forward, bend it and straighten it. The area related to the lips and the mouth is very large, the mouth being involved in sampling, tasting, masticating, speaking, laughing, whistling, singing, and so on. To sum up, we may say that the size of the area is proportional to the skills that the motor cortex regulates and not to the size of the limb or member it commands.

Do you know that localization of learned functioning in right-handed people is found in the left hemisphere only? Or that functions that need little or no learning—those for which simple growth and maturity are enough—are located symmetrically in both hemispheres? Functions for which a long and elaborate apprenticeship is essential are located exclusively in the left hemisphere for right-handed people.

Remember that the "Broca area" for speech is on the left side of the brain for right-handed people and on the other side only for the small number of true left-handed ones.

When I am presented with a trouble in function, I make a special effort not to think in words. I try not to think logically and in correctly formed sentences. It has become a habit with me to imagine the relevant nervous structures by seeing them with my mind's eye. I imagine a part which produces a flow of fluid. Part of the travel of the fluid is electrical, then becomes chemical, and again electrical. After many transformations the flow will end in a muscular contraction, and the muscular play will result in some apparent outside action involving the body, or parts of it, that will affect or transform the immediate environment. Sometimes I am stuck at a point where I cannot imagine the pattern of the flow, nor the possible obstacles in its way. Then I ask, is the obstacle a diffusion, damping, deviation, loss of impetus, break of continuity, or an impossibility of one of the transformations?

I have found this way of imagining so fruitful that I cannot do without it. It often shows me where my knowledge is insufficient so that I know exactly what I am after and therefore in which books I am likely to find the information. I form a working theory and change it in the light of new observations. This gives me a fair idea of what data I lack and what observations I must add to make the theory work. This mode of thinking is often successful in situations where specialists with greater knowledge than mine have failed. Nobody is omniscient enough to think mechanically. I start each case as if it were my first, and ask myself more questions than any of my assistants or critics ever do.

Nora's sister had been present at the session where Nora could not find her way out of the room. It would have been funny, if it were not so pathetic, that she only then realized how serious the situation was. In the three years of Nora's illness she had believed that it was only "this reading and writing" that had gone wrong, but that otherwise her sister was quite normal. Nora herself felt very silly about her inabilities and smiled in a shamefaced way, excusing herself for her failures. She also felt that she was normal except for the reading and writing, and that she should be able to do what we expected her to do.

It was clear to me and the assistants present at this session that this was not a case in which training or exercising—just repeating the wanted action many times—had a chance of success. A better and deeper understanding of learning and of the age of regression was essential if Nora was to recover her lost functions.

The incident with the doors had proved to me that Nora's body awareness was defective, and at that point I recalled the Broca finding that speech is localized in one hemisphere. I tried to guess where body awareness could be located. Could reading and writing have their localization in both hemispheres or in one only? And, in the latter case, would they follow speech: would they be in the left hemisphere for right-handed people? Or would they be on the side opposite the speech area? Here I needed a working theory, without which I could have no inkling of what experience or detail to look for. But how does one make a theory?

Take the questions I have asked about the localization of the reading and writing functions and guess the answers. You may begin by saying that the reading area in the cortex is where the Almighty put it, and the writing center might be anywhere else. This theory leaves you as helpless as before, and leads to searching for somebody who knows where the reading area happens to be. And when you know where it is, you can then affirm that you know where it is.

In the beginning of my work I actually went through such exercises, and always tested the result by whether it led to an action to be tried. If it led to no action, I rejected the original basis or axiom.

You may try the evolution theory, which is a good self-deceptive way to avoid referring to the Creator. Evolution deals only with laws that happened somehow, evolved, and led to survival. Why survival? Simply because without it nothing would survive. In spite of the ease with which one can ridicule any verbal assertion, evolution is a good guide to historic development, but a poor one for prediction. Nobody can assert the survival of might rather than weakness, great bulk rather than minuteness—and no one can see the aim or direction of evolution. It seems to tend toward increased complexity without ever cutting off the way of retreat to a previously tested organization. The real difficulty in finding working theories for action in evolution is the tremendous amount of time that must elapse before you can make even the simplest prediction. You can never tell who, or what, is the fittest for survival before survival takes place.

Examining many other alternative approaches to theory-building, I hit on what has proved to be a good idea. I focus my thinking on the function which I am examining: say, the gait of a paralyzed leg. I imagine the entire function of walking, from the point of view of the individual as well as from that of the species. I limit myself to one function. In the course of my practice, having to deal with all sorts of dysfunction, I gradually learned quite a bit about the evolution of the nervous system, comparative anatomy, and other related disciplines. The theory of structures, cybernetics, theoretical mechanics and so forth I fortunately knew from thirty years of work as a physicist. I also benefited from twenty years of teaching judo and was therefore in a position to imagine that I had been given the task of constructing a robot which would work like an ideal human being, and to be confident that I could accomplish the task. But even the insignificant degree of construction which I could visualize brought me to reconsider the fundamentals—structure and function, speech and thinking, posture and action—and to arrive at conclusions undermining most of what I knew. Had I failed to arrive at constructive conclusions I would be considered, if not mad, then at least somewhat deranged. I thought so more than once myself, and some of my former academic colleagues shunned my company in the years when I was relinquishing my position as a physicist directing research projects in one country or another, and shifting gradually, laboriously and painfully to bettering human ways of self-direction.

Restricting my attention to one function, I visualized the information that must be gathered from the environment and the mechanisms that can handle it, then the body structure housing the intention to move, and, lastly, the tools that can realize the intention. Finally, I considered the integration of the data from the outside with the continuous changes of position of the body structures.

I tried to clarify for myself the notion of body awareness.

In one's personal history, the mouth is the first organ to be used and to make meaningful contact with the external world, in this case the nipples. It seems likely, therefore, that the mouth is also involved in emotions. Otherwise, why is my loved one a sweetheart, honey, or sugar? Some cultures use terms of endearment borrowed from the next stage of development—the anal—instead of oral terms. *Ma petite crotte* is an endearment to the French. One can imagine, or actually watch, how a baby is helped and helps himself to become aware of his nose, eyes, and the rest of himself. Try to realize what a change of position means to a baby's orientation. I personally believe that the baby lying in his mother's arms to be fed has no experiences other than sensory changes. But these changes of feeling register in his nervous system, are integrated and remembered and determine his ability to act in the future. They form his awareness.

Another very significant step in awareness is distinguishing between right and left. It is difficult to learn the difference; many adults are left with a poor sense of this differentiation and use all sorts of mnemonic tricks when they turn right or left. A corporal becomes hoarse ordering recruits to turn right and finding that more than one turns left. Generally the mistake is not due to inattention or forgetfulness; it is something that recurs much too often to be a slip. You may smile at my stretching the significance of orientation failures and accuse me of building a theory on a flimsy basis. Test yourself. Lie on your back and lift your arms overhead. Stop reading. Go and try.

Did you lift your arms over your head or did you direct them to the ceiling? If the latter, your arms would be horizontal when you are standing, and not overhead. Therefore, *overhead* or "above your head" has a different meaning to you with each position of your head and body; it means one thing in the vertical and another in the horizontal position. But in telling your right from your left it is indifferent whether you are lying or standing. Right is right and left is left, even when you are upside down.

This differentiation is extremely significant—one of the first real differentiations between body awareness and its orientation. Though changes from the prone to the upright position of the head are experienced early, the right and left are very blurred at the beginning. Only in childhood after we have learned to walk are we instructed that we have right and left sides, and still later, how to make left and right turns. If you are a driver, think how hard it can be to retain driving instructions if you are told to turn right . . . then left, and left again, and so on.

Lift your arms overhead again, this time sitting or standing. Do you remember what you did? See whether your spontaneous action has changed. Have your lifted arms the same relation to your body now as when you are lying on your back? Is one experience sufficient for you to learn?

To make my approach to Nora's reeducation clear, I ask you to realize that babies are not taught to write before they can walk properly. How would you teach a one-year-old baby to write "b" and "d" or "m" and "w"? He must be able to tell right from left, up from down, and have mastered other and finer degrees of orientation relative to himself before he can learn to write. Could you conceive a method whereby a five-year-old child could be taught that ———— means a horizontal line?

To write one must sense one's finer movements and relate them to an object outside. The localization of writing is organically interwoven with body awareness and it might not be at all distinguishable from awareness; they must at least be closely related. A baby makes marks on paper or other surfaces with a colored chalk or pencil long before he can read. Only when the marks are written as signs can we take it as writing. I reasoned with myself and decided that the localized reading area on the cortex cannot be far from those of body awareness and writing.

Try to imagine the position of the homunculus on the cortex and guess where the areas of writing and reading ought to be. Is the writing area above or below, and where would you put the reading area, knowing the two others? If you consult an atlas of the brain you can see for yourself that the areas of localization of writing and reading are clustered around that of body awareness.

A hint to help you: when taught to read the index finger is generally used to assist the location of what is to be read. Sacred books were always read with a silver hand, the index finger gliding and indicating word after word. The area you will find lies between the visual cortex and the index finger. See whether you can locate it more precisely.

After debating with myself where a function ought reasonably to be, I always check my conclusion against the writing of a reliable scientist, so that if my conclusion is wrong, I not only know that I am wrong but also which gap in my knowledge directed my thinking erroneously. I find it practically impossible to forget anything I've learned in this manner. Moreover, what I've learned is not another item added to a register of dead knowledge, but a dynamic correction in the process of thinking. It is knowledge that directly and immediately transforms the manner of what I am doing. My action has changed and is more direct, more efficient.

Mistakes: Part of Learning

Several years ago Dr. Abe Kirshner from Sir George William University was invited to Jerusalem University to lecture on the reeducation of backward children. He had read my book *Body and Mature Behavior* and was interested in talking to me. He had observed with some surprise that children who could not learn to write in a class of their own age also had trouble walking along a straight line as well as their peers. This and other observations of Dr. Kirshner's saved many children from being put into homes for backward children.

Several years pass before a child becomes aware of the relative efforts in his fingers, before his body sense can direct his finger to follow what his eyes see. He must learn to program his actions, to be able to start, move, and end a movement making sense. No wonder, therefore, that one skill can be less developed than others. This kind of learning either happens, or it does not. Children who cannot learn to write or read lag behind a little more each year, becoming relatively more backward as other children keep on developing while learning.

In general, neither parents nor teachers know better than

to show examples and insist on imitation. It is amazing that there are not more failures to learn by this method than there are; even so, they are much more frequent than is generally realized. Many a mother knows the agony of discovering that something is wrong with her child and that the methods which work well with other children do not help her child. She may believe that the child lacks will, is not interested, or some other such half-truth. Half-truths are habits of speech mistaken for facts. Maybe her child "has no curiosity." Curiosity is a sign of health in man and in animal. Such a child may be "lazy," but more often he has been made emotionally ill by his immediate environment. It is not rare to find that helping a child of that kind to coordinate his eyes with his fingers elicits the will to learn and saves the child from being classed as backward.

I want you to understand that the solution does not lie in simple training. Repetitions, exhortations, rewards, and punishments do not work any better than in Nora's case.

I had Nora lie on her back on a couch-table so that there would be easy access from all sides. I put a wooden roller with a soft spongy cover behind her nape, thus raising her face to where it would be relative to the body when the person was standing. I put another roller under her knees and moved each leg until the feet were lying toes out, heels close together. I wanted to make her comfortable and more at ease, and to reduce the tonus of the body so that she could detect and recognize very gentle movements. The body arranged thus is supported everywhere and relieved of the usual necessity to react to the pull of gravity. The nervous system gradually stops maintaining the muscles at the normal high level of contraction where they are ready to move at the slightest intention.

To relax Nora further, I put my right hand lightly on her forehead and barely moved it to the left and, even more lightly, moved it back to the right. I repeated, changing the direction of my hand several times, making my movement continually lighter and smaller until it was barely perceptible. Because she felt no coercion, nor any reason for resisting, her body relaxed even more. Her neck muscles became soft and her head moved under the impulse of my hand so smoothly that an onlooker could not tell whether I moved her forehead or she turned her head to move my hand. She relaxed more deeply; her abdomen and then her chest began to heave evenly; she was breathing as a healthy baby.

Her body got warmer, her eyes opened more; her soft breathing was followed with occasional full, deep breaths. Slowly and unobtrusively, I changed the right and left movement of the head to barely perceptible pressure on the top of her head. This pressure, directed longitudinally along the spine, must be done with care, after a lot of practice, if it is not to produce any shearing stresses anywhere in the spine. It produces a further relaxation as the automatic parts of the nervous system find progressively less weight in the members of the body to react to. When this action is done well, the patient feels completely weightless and safe and enjoys a kind of nirvana or beatitude. If the patient is conducted and assisted subsequently in getting up so that there are no sudden jerks or efforts, her feeling of weightlessness, together with a clear sensation of being taller, may last for hours and even days.

Nora improved nicely and I was almost lulled into outright

optimism. From day to day I varied my techniques slightly, starting each day with another limb or part of the trunk, until I had gone over her whole body. At the end of each session I touched one part, say the ear, and said, "This is the right ear"; then the shoulder, "This is the right shoulder"—and so on through all the parts of her right side. For several days running, I talked only of her right side during these sessions: I intentionally avoided the word "left." If she happened to lift her left hand when asked to lift the right, I would say, "No, this is the other side, lift the right."

You will perhaps have trouble believing that after a week of this training, when I asked her to lie on her stomach, we had to start all over again. To her mind "the right" was not carried with her body, but was projected and linked to the couch or to the wall. When she changed her position, her right side was not in the same relative place and neither were the other parts of the room, nor was I in the same place. We had to start again, to repeat the old procedure with her lying on her back, and later turn her onto her stomach again.

We do not realize the amount of learning in childhood we must do before we can carry our system of reference; we do it by kinesthetic sensory recall and imagination. Thus, when I crossed Nora's right leg over the left, for instance, she referred to her left leg as right, because in her mind it was on the same side as her right hand or hip, or was similarly related to some other clue on the couch. It took about two months of daily work before Nora correctly appreciated right and left in all positions, with her arms crossed one way and her legs the other, while lying on her stomach, on her side, and so on.

Have you asked yourself why this sort of instruction had to be preceded by the reduction of tension and the relaxation techniques? We seldom think of how we learn the skill of relating to our bodies or to the walls around us, nor do we realize that our orientation is often far from perfect. Many of us carry a mixture of reference into adult life. We are not always clear what "hands overhead" means: the exercise in the previous chapter showed that it means one arrangement when lying and another when standing. In the same way, we fail to appreciate what we mean by childhood. One is a child not only because he is smaller and lighter but essentially because of his childish attitude. The ability to learn a skill such as right-left orientation needs the childish state of mind, the ability to play while learning the ability to pay attention, without intending to learn. It also needs, among other requirements, the ability to feel differences; that is, the ability to distinguish between one sensation and another very similar one. It needs attention with intention. The child does not exercise in the sense a grown-up does, by repeating an action in order to improve it. The child's attention is directed by curiosity, which is innate in all living things. Repetition in a small child is more often due to the pleasure the act evokes and to its novelty, than to any intent to improve. This state of mind goes together with total satisfaction of oneself and excitement and the absence of desires which tense the body and the spirit. The simple mood, posture, and movement are conditions for learning—which is also growth.

The obvious is not always simple or easy to understand. Sensitivity decreases with strain. Children cannot tense their muscles as powerfully as grown-ups can; this makes for greater sensitivity in children and better learning. Suppose a man carries a forty-pound load on his back. How much weight can be added to the load before the man becomes aware of the addition? In other words, what is his sensitivity? If a fly lands on the load and then soars off again, the man will certainly not notice. Will he know if two flies land? Our sensations function in such a way that about one-fortieth of the load must be taken away or added for us to become aware of a change in our effort to carry the weight. Because the efforts a child can make are smaller, he becomes aware of much smaller changes. A young child is more sensitive; in getting used to smaller changes, he grows stronger and less sensitive. You can see why it is necessary to reduce muscular tonus or tension so that a person can again distinguish delicate changes and thus increase the acuity of his sensory functions. Without the ability to sense fine differences we take too large steps, and soon, with only a few big changes, reach the limit of human capacity. A sick person cannot take great changes and cannot be helped by rough methods. The learning of a child lasts many years; the relearning of a severely traumatized adult lasts many months.

During the nearly two months before Nora knew everything one needs to know, in our state of culture, about right and left of one's body, there were days when I thought we had reached the end of the training. Then, next day, I would find it necessary to start all over again. But the relapses became smaller and rarer until I could move to the next step.

If I did not learn to detect minute changes from moment to moment and day to day I could not continue the endless repetitions of the training. I teach my assistants to see progress even during relapses. In the work that I do, I have to remind myself of familiar phenomena and look at them afresh, as if I had never known them. In this way I find solace in difficult moments and insight into the case at hand. People forget that to master flowing handwriting requires many years of practice. Looking for progress every week, one can hardly see change unless he concentrates on minor details.

In normal life we also observe intelligent functions coexisting with very inadequate ones. I know a world-famous musician who is unable to use a screwdriver or repair a fuse. Nora could be taken for an intelligent woman based on her conversation, which was couched in sensible and well-constructed phrases.

Sometimes we wonder whether something is wrong with a friend, but we are unable to put our finger on our concern. Later, the inkling we had proves to be well-founded. My assistants are fascinated when their attention is called to something in the attitude or posture of a patient which they know they knew but cannot place in their minds. They learn to identify the vague inkling immediately when it is pointed out as part of the problem. It is exhilarating to be able to verbalize such a finding for the first time. Eventually, this ability becomes a habit of thought, second nature. My students often remark on what I fail to observe, and I have benefited by their questions and by the freshness of their observations.

Soon it was time to start Nora with reading and writing. There is a better reason for starting with reading than just the customary order of words. Writing is almost unthinkable without first seeing words.

We were alone, and I invited Nora to sit on a comfortable

chair. Even though she had accepted the presence of my assistants during other sessions, I knew that she was unwilling to expose her inadequacies now. Their presence would make her nervous and falsify my judgment of her achievements. I had hope that after an initial period of hesitation her reading would improve; any sort of reading is an improvement on no reading at all.

I was prepared for the possibility that Nora's eyesight had deteriorated and would present an extra problem. I brought out her glasses and practically had to put them on for her. Next I showed her a text with print large enough to be read without glasses by a person with poor eyesight; but she strained her eyes and exclaimed, "I cannot see a thing! Do you not see that I cannot?" She was excited and stiff and took her glasses off, trembling and almost crying. I comforted her, meanwhile thinking that her focusing was wrong and that the eyes did not converge on the same point. There may have been further damage to her brain, and it was impossible to interpret the retinal information. There may also have been changes in the cornea, or a cataract, or even changes in the vitreous humor of the eyeballs.

Afterwards I discussed this problem with a very intelligent ophthalmologist, who examined Nora thoroughly, dismissed most of my conjectures, and assured me that my patient's eyes form a correct picture.

Two puzzles remained for me to solve. Since Nora could not read I had no way to check her ability to focus. And I was concerned about her ability to see in three dimensions. People who have never seen pictures cannot visualize the subject photographed from a two-dimensional picture. They do not know which way to turn a photo; children often fail to recognize the images of their own mothers. To see what we see in a photograph we need experience in childhood. A year-old baby would tear or throw away mother's picture, clearly failing to find any connection. It takes time to learn to see the third dimension on a flat picture and to construe the image of a person out of lines and dots.

I saw Nora again only to be shocked. She had her glasses in her bag, took them out and tried for ten minutes to put them on—attempting the most unthinkable approaches, none of them accomplishing the object of putting the bows behind her ears. There are four possible positions for glasses in space; only one allows us to fix them on our faces. If you do not recognize the unique position as the one you seek, you may fumble and even turn back to the wrong position and finally give up in despair as Nora did.

I was annoyed with myself for not having realized that even the transfer from body awareness to external objects needs training, and that orientation of objects relative to ourselves does not come from nowhere. I now saw much more clearly that I had to discipline myself to a much slower rate of learning than the present one, which seemed slow enough to me. Nora would move the glasses with the bows closed or pointing away from her face and wait half a minute or more, then smile, recognizing that position as faulty. She could not, however, correct the position if the glasses were handed over to her. In the end I turned them in the right direction and gave them to her to put on. Later I had to spend some time on this movement. I was also surprised that when she happened to find the glasses on the table set just right to be put on, she did so without any trouble.

A baby playing with glasses would have the same experience, until the day when by chance they happen to be posi-
tioned so that putting them on is simple and easy. We may
think that the baby has chosen this efficient position from
among the faulty ones, but when a baby chooses in that way
he is no longer a baby but a clever child.

With the glasses on in the right way, I again put a book in
front of Nora. This time I did not ask her to read; I asked her
simply to look at the two pages in front of her. After she
stared at the pages, I asked her to close her eyes and say any
word that came to her mind. I wrote down the page number
and the words she said, sometimes after a long silence. In the
end I had listed about fifty significant words; I mean names
or verbs, adjectives or adverbs, and not just *ein* or *das*. Later
I spent hours locating those words on the pages, and I became convinced that all the words were on the left-hand
page, about a third of the page from the bottom and about
three words from the end of a line. I was exhilarated. She did
read words but did not know where she read them. She
looked at one place but obviously saw clearly a second place.
I cannot describe what I felt at my discovery. It turned out
that I had guessed correctly and had designed the test with
insight.

I marvel at how children learn to read. It is much more
difficult than one thinks. The important thing, however, is
the insight it gives into what and how to plan education, and
why some people fail to master this skill. The wonder is that
the majority succeed.

I tried to identify myself with my patient. What was she
actually doing when she intended to read? Where did she
intend or expect to read? Did she intend to read the first

word of the page, and then fail to accommodate or focus? Or did she simply become anxious and fail to direct her gaze, allowing herself to look far into the distance, as though looking at infinity, her eyes not converging at all? Did she see the words she said with her better eye, or with both? How on earth was I going to find out?

In the following pages I will tell you how I found out, and share my satisfaction with the progress of Nora's case. I am keen to understand our ways of functioning so that we can learn to make our lives easier and more enjoyable. From what I have told you up to now, you will see that each one of us can improve his own orientation and body awareness. It is not easy to see incompleteness in one's own functioning except by comparing oneself with others. It is easy to realize that someone runs or swims faster than I do, and there are many actions that somebody performs better than I. But if I can improve my orientation and body awareness, then I achieve a fundamental change which can better any of the actions making up my life.

Would you like to conduct a personal experiment? Standing or walking slowly, examine where you look and how. Do you look mostly forward and ignore anything to your left and your right? Do you listen to the space behind you? Do you normally sense what is above you without something attracting your attention from above? Well-organized, adroit people do not focus continuously on the ground they tread but only from time to time. Most of the time their senses are diffused, and they see almost everything from left to right. Their ears hear what happens behind them. An animal or a solitary man in the jungle would not survive a day if he were not aware of most of the space around him. The fact that personal security is assured collectively in our society, and not by each person, does not mean that our senses need not function properly. The quality of the life we live still depends mostly on the condition of our personal equipment.

4

Improving vs. Curing

Because we begin learning to read at the top left corner of a page, I realized that Nora did intend to read the first words there. This part of her reading was not affected, except that she had an incorrect appreciation of what she was doing. Normally what is fed back from the environment to the nervous system gradually decreases the error of the initial shot in the blue until we see the desired point with the greatest clarity. In modern parlance, the feedback from the environment did not produce the correction asymptotically. I am not sure that you will find it easy to follow my argument in these terms, but I am so convinced that I would achieve nothing at all if I relied on explanations that I can only tell you what I did and leave the reasoning to you.

Take a drinking straw, put one end in your mouth and support the middle of it with the tips of your thumb and forefinger. Look at the tips of your fingers and not the straw. Move your fingers slowly away from your lips to the middle of the straw, and then slowly back to your lips. If you continue for a couple of minutes and if your sight is adequate, at a certain moment you will see two straws ahead of your fingertips bifurcating at an angle, the size of which depends on the distance between your fingers and your mouth. The straw should be held motionless and straight. Once you have managed to see a bifurcation you will continue to see it more and more clearly. You will now see two distinct straws, one deviating to the right and one to the left of the real straw. When your fingers are nearer your mouth, the impression is created of two straws as long as the real straw. When your fingers are in the middle of the straw, the two straws you see are also half their original size, but the angle between them has changed.

Next, close your right eye and you will see only the left-deviated straw image; close your left eye and you will see only the right. When your fingers are near your mouth, your eyes converge almost to the point of crossing, as when you look at the tip of your nose. Each eye sees the straw at the prolongation of the straight line (or ray) from the eye to the fingertip, hence the crossing of the straws or the bifurcation of the images of the straw in the two eyes.

After more practice with your straw, sliding the finger support farther and farther away from your mouth and back, you will see that the farther from the mouth the smaller the bifurcated images of the straw. When at last the fingers support the very end of the straw two different images appear: one going from the farther end of the straw to the right of the mouth and the other to the left.

I conducted this test with Nora in order to see her eyes converging and diverging as her fingertips moved nearer her mouth and away from it. When she confirmed seeing two straws, by observing the position of the fingertips under the straw I could also appreciate whether both eyes converged or diverged by the same amount. I could see by the position and movement of her eyes whether she reported truly about the bifurcation, and also the direction of errors when they were made.

Because the straw is a detector of how the eyes focus, I knew what she was seeing and could appreciate whether her eyeballs moved as normally as they should. Checking it on myself, I realized that despite good eyesight I did not see straightaway what I saw after a few trials, so I continued trying with Nora.

Once the use of the device was understood and tested, I used it to improve the convergence of her eyes for better focusing. When the convergence of the eyes for nearer seeing is improved, the divergence of the eyes for seeing at a distance is equally improved. Moving the fingertips nearer to the mouth and away from it makes for focusing near and far; the eyes move inward or converge for near vision and move apart or diverge for distance.

If you try this device for yourself you will observe that you gradually see more and better as you go along. When later your fingers reach the end of the straw, the extended bits of image become smaller and disappear. You see two images of the straw stretching from its end to either side of your face. At first before your eyes focus effectively the images are only barely recognizable for what they are. As the focusing of your eyes becomes more precise, you see the images almost as clearly as the bifurcations before.

Having this wonderful toy in my arsenal, I put my patient through a thorough examination and subsequent training. When I brought her to the point of seeing the two images directed from the end of the straw to either side of her face, I was sure that she focused ideally at the end of the straw, and that if I put the tip of the straw on a printed word on a page her eyes were ideally focused to see that word. If she could not read it then, her eyes could not be blamed and there must be trouble much "higher" in the brain.

It has happened over and over again that incapacitated or paralyzed people whom I have helped were unruffled the first time they succeeded at an act which they had lost the ability to perform. In my presence they think, "He made me do it" or "I cannot do it—he did it with me." Only when they do the same thing on their own initiative at home do they finally admit improvement. I used to think them ungrateful, as if they did not want to admit that they had succeeded through my skill. Later I found that unless they can do the recovered act without thinking about it, they do not feel that they are "cured." They want simply to have the intention and do the action without knowing what and how they do it. In short, people are so ignorant of the way they learn to do things that they believe any awareness of a conscious effort is an indication that they are not normal. To most people, life is something that works automatically, and if it does not, they have to be cured.

You may be interested in the following letter from a student of my three-year seminar at San Francisco:

> After reading your book for the fourth time and re-reading Selye's book *The Stress of Life,* I am beginning to realize that what you are teaching has unlimited possibilities in the field of medicine. I can hardly keep still!

The thing that finally brought it all home to me was the realization of the importance of the word "function." I have always had the idea that life was a "thing" to be manipulated, but it is not really so. Life is a process, a function, something that is always moving and to try to make it stand still, to define it, or to "cure" it as a stationary object, is completely absurd. The process is to be corrected, reorganized and then, if there is a defect of structure, the new process goes about restructuring it to better fit the function. Well, that is the way it looks to me right now and the potential is enormous!

You can see from the writer's observations why a crippled person can hardly be expected to realize from the first few successes that she has changed and is functioning better. She is not "cured." She expects to be exactly as she was before her trauma. To be cured means return to her past mode of functioning. But life is a process, and an irreversible process at that.

Nora wanted or expected cure, not improvement. "Improvement" is a gradual bettering which has no limit. "Cure" is a return to the previously enjoyed state of activity which need not have been excellent or even good. The habitual and familiar we do not question; improvement we grade. The former is the automatic background of our system; the latter is the foreground of our awareness. The two are different dimensions. One is an atavistic sensation; the other is a learned knowledge that gives us freedom of choice—which is the major prerogative of Homo sapiens.

Talking without Words

I am sure that I learned more through our common experience than Nora did. After nearly forty years of experience, I can observe a patient's movement and gather so much information that my students are often speechless, or ask who told me that, when I reveal something. People prefer to believe in miracles, such as guidance by the spirit of a dead doctor or some other farfetched explanation, rather than to verbalize their inner sensations.

I directed Nora to look at the end of the straw adjusted in length to normal reading distance (25cm) and placed on a word, and asked her to say a word crossing her mind. When she saw the word at the end of the straw for the first time, her lips opened and she dropped the straw from her mouth. Her first movement was to catch the straw and not to speak the word she saw. I knew that she saw the word and would have uttered it were her mouth free. Then the word was gone. In a flash I knew that she saw the word but did not *read* it; I remembered that she had never said "I cannot read," but always "I cannot see." Not seeing the difference, I had concentrated on her reading problem while her real problem was, first, seeing, and only later reading. The transformation into words of the letters she saw was the difficulty, not uttering the words or seeing the letters.

Soon enough she was able to say the word at the end of the straw, and after making about twenty trials, I showed her that all her guesses were correct. Since I wanted her to express verbally what she felt and realized, I refrained from saying "You did read" or "You can see." She was not moved at all by her first success nor by the next few. I saw once more that we usually distort facts by our own conviction. Facts are not independent of the observer. I would have jumped with joy to realize that I could read after years of being unable to do so. Nora said the words at the end of the straw, but obviously did not sense inwardly, or did not realize, what she had accomplished. She said nothing. Only later, after a large number of successes and after I explained that this was not just a fluke, did she seem to agree that we had achieved something.

The working of our thoughts is an endless wonder. The realization I have just related was behind my first idea of putting the straw in her mouth. Dr. Kirshner, whom I have already mentioned, and to whom I have shown the technique with the straw, asked, "Why in the mouth?"

On the spur of the moment I retorted, "Do we not read with our mouths?" He understood much of my reasoning, but my students did not, and I have already confessed my own muddled thinking about reading and seeing.

Nora and I had our "aha" experience, our discovery, at the same time. To help you out of the confusion I may have created above, here is the core of it. We first learn to speak, and only after speaking fairly well do we learn to read. Here we have to establish a fluent connection between what we see and what we understand. But for a long time we utter, and are taught to utter, what we see. Many people move their lips while reading as long as they live. Some have never been able to read faster than they can verbalize what they see. We can never learn to read aloud a thousand words a minute, as we cannot speak at that rate. Yet, without knowing what we do, we find a way of dissociating the scanning of the print from speaking, and so we learn to read fast; the seeing is directed to the conceptualizing or understanding, bypassing speech altogether. This is not an easy task and very few achieve real perfection unaided. We find all grades among readers. Some, like praying nuns, move their lips and speak their prayers voicelessly. Others have not reached even that differentiation and read even their daily papers aloud; in these cases, the reading age is that of a child after two or three years of reading. You may think that I exaggerate. Well, examine yourself even if you have taken lessons in fast reading. See whether you can count money fast without talking at all, counting directly with your intelligence. This you have not learned, and you probably continue to count like a peasant who never had the leisure to read directly with his eyes.

When I was about ten years old, I watched the father of a schoolmate pour the coins from his purse onto the table, spread them evenly, and shovel them back into his purse. He then wrote in his cash ledger so many coins of the larger denomination, so many coins of the next, and so on, and wrote the total at the bottom. I stood and gaped at him, not believing what I had seen; I asked my friend whether I had imagined it. He said his father could always count coins spread out more or less in one layer simply by glancing at them for a few seconds.

Later, I knew a sect of Jewish mystics, the cabalists, who dedicate their being to the higher spheres of knowledge. To attain the wisdom and power of God they teach that a man needs all the time he can spare; they therefore learn to satisfy all earthly needs in the nick of time so as to increase their free time for heightening their level of being. The father of my schoolmate grew up in such a yeshiva.

If you contemplate what you read, you will realize that words are not thoughts, but cues to thoughts; the same word can call up different thoughts even in the same person, let alone in others. Communication is not exchange of thinking but only a hopeful attempt; I cannot claim to have convinced anybody to think in a way contrary to his habit of thought, no matter how I have worded my effort. But creating an atmosphere of understanding makes it possible to recreate the content of the words in the mind of a real friend or loved and loving person. In spite of words being the sole and general means of communication, they have no meaning, because of having too many, and because the ways of using them are infinite.

I should perhaps make clear what some of you have already guessed. Much of what I do in my lessons involves no talking; still, I talk like everybody else most of the time. It would make a patient suspicious and restless if I did not talk as though I were on speaking terms with him. I invite the person—whom I consider as a pupil rather than as a patient —to assume a convenient position, such as lying on the back or on the stomach, or kneeling on a soft pad. During a series of lessons with a pupil, who may be a violinist who does not improve in spite of diligent practice, or an actor, or somebody having chronic back pains, the variety of positions is great and seemingly endless. In the nearly forty years of applying my system or technique of functional integration, a pupil rarely needs to receive more lessons than he is old. Thus somebody of thirty years of age will learn sufficiently in thirty lessons to be free of the pain or difficulty which brought him to me. He will not have reached his potential limit but will be in a state of continuing to grow or to improve, if you prefer, by his own power or by my group technique, which is known as Awareness Through Movement.

Many people have difficulty in understanding how the same theory, or system, can be nonverbal when I teach one individual, and yet involve speech in a group session where speaking is of necessity the only means of contact. In the nonverbal teaching I use my hands, and this is a sensory experience. In the groups, the same result is obtained by using speech, though not in the usual way of requiring people to obey instructions. They are not expected to achieve anything; they only have to pay attention to the sensory experience of attempting to move. Thus both techniques are essentially sensory experiences.

It is a sad truth that the verbal method of communication cannot be more than a clue. The objective cannot be acquired by talking or communicating. The subject of the communication must be a thought imagined, felt, sensed, invented, or conceived. We communicate by talking about anything we have heard or read, seen or felt, thought or dreamed. Talking is nothing but communicating what has already come into being, though only an instant before.

I tell you all this so that you may appreciate that during the first two months the verbal aspect of Nora's treatment involved only greetings and a few words to move her into the situation which I later corrected with my hands. My hands are so trained that they give me a sensory report of what the pupil feels and at the same time convey information that can be acted upon even if it is not understood. The pupil reacts not through understanding but spontaneously, resisting or yielding to my pressure or pull, or withdrawing when a painful area is touched.

Using the straw, as described earlier, involved no talking, but only sticking the end of the straw in Nora's mouth and putting her index finger and thumb into the position of supporting it. Until the end of the lesson, only the invitation to look at the fingertips was spoken. I did not ask "What do you see?" Instead I would say, "How many straws can you see here or there—one, two, or three?" "Are they all of the same quality, that is, brightness; is any of them more real?" Nothing more was necessary.

I tell you this because I want you to know that I experienced difficulties when she read without realizing that she did so. After some practice I could see roughly what each eye did as I watched her eyes moving to follow her fingertips. But this did not tell me what she felt. While her focusing was improving, my appreciation of the change in her eye function was growing, but still I did not know whether she saw with both eyes equally. Was one eye dominant and the other only an auxiliary? The better eye, the dominant one, should see the virtual image of the straw branching to the opposite side. It was unlikely that she was able to tell one side from the other, or to become aware of such a fine difference;

indeed, the auxiliary eye may have been seeing a fainter virtual image, but was still seeing something.

To discover what was really happening, I used a dark pink drinking straw that matched a plastic colored sheet. If I placed the colored sheet on the side where the image of the bifurcation of the straw was faint, the image would disappear altogether, being indistinguishable from the background of the same color; and the disappearance would provoke some sort of visible reaction from Nora. If I placed it on the other side, opposite the dominant eye, the image of the straw would stand out by contrast even brighter than before or at least as clear, and so be distinguishable to Nora. An experienced observer can tell by the look of the eyes whether the person actually sees. The eyes stop focusing and move apart when one does not see what is expected at one's fingertips.

Many people have one eye which sees better than its mate, and Nora had, in fact, one eye considerably stronger than the other. An eye tends to focus so that the image is formed on the macula of that eye; the macula is a small area which enables one to see finer details than does the rest of the retina. Glasses are usually adjusted to correct the accommodation of each eye separately to the best sight obtainable. For absolutely perfect vision, one lens of the glasses would have to be prismatic, so that the more corrected eye can be focused to the same point as the better or less corrected eye. In practice, this is too expensive and difficult. Therefore, glasses only rarely eliminate all the errors of vision.

Having to cope with so many difficulties at the same time, I tried to eliminate the ones I could. Learning to read with a damaged brain is difficult enough for a patient. I hoped to obtain an objective conviction that Nora's eyes had a clear picture of the print in front of her; hence the care to eliminate all possible hindrance.

From the moment the end of the straw and the fingers on which her eyes were focused reached a printed word on a page, it took only about two weeks before Nora could read aloud. I was able to record her reading aloud four pages in half an hour. This is fair enough, considering that reading aloud slows one down.

This achievement felt like a triumph because I had overcome difficulties which I had not even suspected. For example, when she finished reading the first page she stopped, obviously at a loss to know where to read next. She returned the straw to the top of the page she had just finished, and as content of the top of the page was naturally not connected with the last line, she was bewildered and embarrassed. Many trials and rehearsals were necessary before she learned to continue by reading the top of the next page.

Even turning the right-hand page did not come by itself, and I confess I was surprised at this. I can appreciate that a small child learning to read may need repeated instruction before turning the page by himself. I believed that imitation would occur naturally, especially with a person who read for many years before forgetting how to read, and I took it for granted that the page difficulties would not arise.

There were other surprises. From the beginning, the straw pointing at a word was moved to the next word on the right, and then back to the left of the next line, so that the end of it would stop at each word until it was read aloud. When I gave Nora the straw (later replaced by a pencil) to indicate the words being read by herself, there was a remarkable difference; whether she indicated the spot to be read depended on whether she held the pencil with the right or the left hand. We obviously learn more than we know or remember learning. It seems that even common sense has to be learned as well as everything that comes naturally.

From the moment Nora saw the word at the end of the straw to the moment I felt her fit to use a pencil to guide her own reading herself took some time. I will describe for you the procedure of those lessons. I sat on a chair to the left of her chair. I put my right hand under her left arm and reached her wrist, put the open book in her left hand and wrapped my hand around hers to help her hold the book in the proper position. With my left hand I held the straw between her lips. In this way, I could feel with my right arm and hand the slightest changes going on in her; I could detect the slightest halt of breathing the minute it occurred, the very moment I had to stop moving the straw until she could take courage, reorganize herself, and get ready to go on. It was a kind of symbiosis of the two bodies—I felt any change in her mood, and she felt my determined, peaceful, noncoercive power. I did not rush her, but would read the words out loud the instant I felt her stiffen with anxiety and lose grip. Gradually I had to read less often. At moments I found her reading better than mine when we encountered double-barreled German words of twenty-five or thirty letters; she could read such words effortlessly where I had to strain and slow down. But also, every now and then she would be tripped by words like *und* or *auf* or *ein*.

There were also difficulties I had anticipated which did not occur. For instance, I had thought that holding something between the lips would make it very difficult to read aloud.

It turned out to be of no consequence, and I remembered myself speaking with a cigarette in my mouth, and English friends who were born with pipes in their mouths. Since I was supporting the straw, there was no difficulty at all.

When I felt that I could give the straw into her hand and let her point to the words and lines to read, she often dropped in the middle of a line to the one below without noticing it. Obviously, she was just saying what she was seeing, without perceiving the content. She could as well have been reading Chinese. I changed the book and looked for one in which there were stories with little descriptive text. This way the narrative facilitated her retention. I would make funny remarks and her laughter would show that she understood the content. From time to time I would pretend not to know the meaning of a German word and she would explain it to me. This device served as a check on her attention to the content as well as giving her the authority of a teacher. I then began to think of weaning her from her dependence on me and equalizing our status to that of two humans conversing and reading together. This gave her real pleasure and the reading could now be left to her.

It was time to start writing. In the light of all that had happened, I wanted to make the sequence of learning to write clear enough to forestall most of the pitfalls and surprises. My students also surprised me, in that some of them seemed to remember learning to read and write at the same time. Long ago I learned that it is too much to expect a human being to foresee the unknown so fully that nothing is a surprise.

I thought there could not be a more gradual passage to

writing than giving Nora a ball-point pen to guide her read-ing instead of the straw which we had been using. I hoped that she would hold it with three fingers as for writing, but instead she held it like an instrument to work with. To illus-trate, I tried to make her use her index finger instead of the pen, but when she tried to stretch her index finger and at the same time close the other fingers into a fist, her index finger bent itself into a hook.

I decided then to continue with the reading for a few days. The first and second day everything proceeded uneventfully as before. On the third day Nora's reading was so good that I had to read only two or three words per page for her. Suddenly, I saw a line being drawn below the line she was reading. She was holding the pen as we hold a writing instru-ment. I looked at her and she realized she had drawn a line between two lines in the book. "When will I learn to write?" Nora asked, looking very happy. I was happy, too, that I had respected my policy of never pushing a pupil into a new act before he stumbles on it or to something near it himself. A new desire or action is an indication of growing health.

"Would you like to start now?" I asked her.

"Ich habe angst—I am afraid," she answered. I took care not to betray my keen expectation of what she would say next; I knew she would tell me something important. I always wait, when undertaking nonverbal work, until the body pat-tern, or more correctly the motor cortex pattern connected with anxiety is resolved. This happens when the pupil thinks of a way of doing something he did not do for many years or maybe never did at all. She thought of the writing she had not done for several years. Obviously, there was little or no anxiety evoked now by the thought of writing.

"I always had anxiety," she continued. "I had it all my life. I remember I had *angst* since I was six. I was afraid of being late to school, I was afraid of being late to school . . ." she repeated.

"Were you ever late?" I asked.

"I was never late to school, but all my life I had dreams of being late to school, and used to wake up shivering with *angst*. I was never late all my life but I still dream of being late to school."

"You are not at school now. What made you think of what you told me? There is no school here."

"Oh yes, it is like a school here."

I remembered now that Nora was always half an hour early for our appointments but it had never occurred to me that this was so important a key to her life. I believed that I was a superobserver—I have told you how I taught observation to my students! For over three months Nora had been half an hour early every day and I had taken it for granted and observed nothing. I still think of myself as a good observer, but certainly not a Sherlock Holmes, as I did originally. The ancestor after whom I was named by Jewish custom used to say, "Modesty is knowing thy place." I have had more than one such lesson to learn in my life.

When Nora told me simply about her anxiety, it seemed to come out of the blue, but it did not. The effects of my work alter the inhibition and excitation in the cortex, which is reflected through muscular flabbiness or contraction. The emotional content associated with the habitual attitude is deprived of its material support and the person becomes aware of the emotion. As he becomes aware of the emotional content linked with his body pattern, through the reduction of the superfluous intensity of contraction, his state is that of peacefulness and ease and he expresses his feelings calmly. There is usually an increase of the sense of well-being which lasts for some time.

Considering that Nora suddenly felt she could tell me about her anxiety and that she held the pen in the writing position of her own accord, I thought it timely to begin recovering her writing ability. Recovery is not the right word, since the part of the motor cortex where writing is organized and directed was not in a state to perform as before. The better word is "recreating" a writing ability.

As before, I avoided rushing her or evoking anxiety by mentioning writing. Just saying "Now we will try writing" would have been enough to produce the familiar blank expression in her eyes. At the same time, her body would have tensed and she would almost certainly have defended herself with "But I cannot." Her way of saying "I cannot" carried the conviction that I could not possibly fail to see that she could not. There was a note of astonishment, too, which meant "How can you say that when you can see for yourself?"

I therefore put a sheet of paper on the table, gave her the pen she had used before, and with another, drew three parallel vertical lines about a centimeter apart. I pushed the sheet over to Nora and invited her to draw what she saw. She touched the paper with the pen three times, producing three ticks faintly resembling the sign signifying "It has been seen and approved."

I thought it was not too bad; she had reproduced no parallel vertical lines but had made the same number of applications of pen to the paper as I had; there were three marks, not two or four. When I drew three horizontal lines parallel to each other, about one centimeter apart, she made marks even closer to mine: there were three small horizontal markings, one after the other, the second a little lower than the first and a bit to its right, and the third marking similarly made. It matched more closely and had more common features with mine than her vertical attempt. When I drew a triangle she imitated by making just three dots; she made four dots for the quadrangle I drew. To imitate the angle I formed, she made two touches of the pen, with no meaningful relation. All I can say is that somehow Nora made the same number of applications to the paper I did while drawing. Otherwise, the situation looked quite hopeless, except that she remained composed. I did nothing to show either dissatisfaction or approval.

Remembering that she could not use her index finger to guide her reading, and thinking of the long time children spend on following the calligraphy in copybooks, I was downhearted. I saw that Nora's body awareness was quite crude, and certainly not delicate enough for writing. In writing, there are frequent changes of direction in moving the pencil or the pen. The duration of movements in one direction and its opposite must be sufficiently equalized. To recreate all this would take a lot of time and ingenuity. I needed to plan procedures from mere ideas, with no more definite and effective means of realization. I would be satisfied if I could get her to sign her name, signatures being an obvious necessity without which a cultured person's life is difficult and awkward.

I now had to travel to teach and lecture abroad on dates fixed before I had started with Nora. I told her that we would make a break, that we had achieved a great deal, and that it was time for us both to have a rest. She agreed to return home, and we decided that she would come back to Israel when she felt she wanted to continue.

The day before leaving she came to say good-bye to all my students. She behaved like a self-confident person, spoke with ease, even with elegance. She was not the patient we remembered from the first session. Everybody felt a sense of achievement, and her simple and sincere thanks made everyone react as to an adult friend. I felt grateful to her for becoming a somebody, and not a pupil, or patient, as we knew her. She left unaccompanied, except that we put her on the plane.

6

Sensing to Understand

A few months after my return to Israel, I was informed that Nora intended to come again to work with me. I was glad to hear from her for several reasons. It was obvious that she felt healthy enough to wish to write, and I felt that she would make faster progress now because I had been thinking of ways to proceed in case she returned.

One morning Nora walked in looking friendly, self-possessed, and well. She told us that she had come by herself and that she could read the signs everywhere. I did not ask whether she had tried writing, but I invited her to take off her shoes as usual and lie on the couch. I then examined her body from the toes to the top of the head. She expanded, relaxed, and left in good spirits.

Next day as she lay on the couch, I started moving the tip of my right index finger in the direction from the head to the feet. I might mention here that I work with my pupils as they come from the street. They never take off anything besides coat, glasses, and shoes. I made very small movements, each stroke of my finger just several centimeters long. I covered her face with such strokes, her forehead, cheeks, throat, chest, abdomen, legs, feet, arms, and hands. Later, the back of her head, the nape of her neck, and the rest of her body were treated likewise. I repeated the same thing for three sessions. She was silent and so was I, but I had to struggle against an itching desire to ask what she thought I was doing. I wondered that she obviously did not find my action odd. Anyway, she was very quiet and let me continue with my strokes, which began to feel very silly to me. At long last she asked, "Is this a line?" referring to the last stroke. "Yes, it is a line from the top downward—*von oben nach unten.*" I kept making my little strokes and saying with each one of them, "This is a line from up downward."

After a few dozen of these I said with each stroke, "That is also a 1 [one]," and again, after a series of strokes, "Maybe it is a printed letter l," and later, adding a dot to the stroke, I suggested, "It might be an i." I realized that people can have a sensory experience and have no awareness of it. A sensory stimulation is really not an experience, just a sensory stimulation. There is no meaning to it before there is an internal query as to what one feels. Unless one looks for a meaning, there is none in the stimulation and none in the sensation of the stimulation.

I tried to find other instances of the same kind. Are we all like that, or only Nora, because of her trauma? I suddenly remembered that I had a pair of shoes which felt comfortable at the start yet caused discomfort at the small toe by the end of the day. I took off the shoe and was surprised to see the toe bleeding—a blister formed by constant slight pressure had burst. Only when the rubbing continued on raw flesh did I become aware of pain. If I could be stimulated for a whole day without asking questions, then why should Nora behave differently, when my strokes were certainly less harsh on her than the pressure on my toes? Stimulations below the threshold of pain have no significance without awareness; awareness gives them meaning. Or maybe the discernment of meaning means awareness.

What about dental cavities? When did you become aware of something wrong in the tooth? When did you feel pain? Was it when your tongue happened to discover a hole in what had been a smooth surface? But the destructive process may have lasted months before you knew anything. So you, too, can be stimulated without asking questions. How long does it take before one knows that a gallstone has formed, or a kidney stone? It takes years of abnormal stimulations which do nothing to make us aware of them, provided they are not too sudden, rough, or painful. Nora's strokes were just like that.

What humbles me is that I devised the method and found in the product of my own mind something that I did not put into it. Or maybe I did, but did not know that I was doing it. Is knowing awareness? A certain kind of knowing certainly is; the very kind of knowing we are talking about.

After I finished with the strokes downward, I reversed the direction, accompanying each stroke, and later every few strokes, with the explanation, "This is a line from down upward." When Nora at long last asked "Why from down upward?" I told her that only if one watches the stroke can one tell which way it was done. Had I dipped my finger in paint before stroking, the direction of the movement would be hard to establish from the trace left. A stroke down or up is still a line, still a printed letter "l" or a figure "1" or an "i" if a dot is added. Only while performing the movement is the direction noticed above all. On the impression that is left, it is the shape which is noted above all.

Nora laughed at this, and found it very funny. I took her hand, moved it onto her body, and made short strokes with it instead of with my finger. Then I took her index finger and used it to stroke her body, face, or whatever part I could reach. Later, I used her index finger to write strokes on the couch. I thought I could recreate a writing area in the cortex faster than it is formed normally in children. But I had already convinced myself that the steps must not be less gradual, that their order could not be inverted, that none should be omitted, or the time to learn to write would take even longer than it takes a child. As the Hebrew saying puts it, "To teach the young is like writing on paper; to teach the old is like writing on blotting paper."

The stroking came to an end; that is, it became boring to Nora and she stopped being passive and indifferent. She behaved as you would if subjected to such a torture. So long as my procedure was just a stimulation and did not affect her awareness, she could take it. Now that it had meaning, it became boring when repeated aimlessly.

I started making two connected strokes like the letter "n" and three like the letter "m" until she could distinguish them. It took several sessions before she became aware that there were trains of two and three strokes. But we reached the stage of boredom and impatience in about half the time as with the simpler strokes. As before, I moved her hand on her body to do the same movement I had performed, and then I finished by guiding her index finger in making "n" and "m" movements.

It is most likely superfluous to point out that the gradations consisted in moving first the larger parts of the arm, which the apes can move faster and stronger than we can, then going on to specifically human manipulations dealing with the finer muscles of the fingers and the forearm, and then carrying over the sensation of the movement of the body to touching and moving an exterior object. It is a large step to make a body stimulation into a designed movement on a surface of the environment. Just think how simple sensations of movements become meaningful when one can verbalize awareness of the sensation or the movement or both.

In the next few sessions I again used my index finger in a small round movement. Touching Nora and moving my finger clockwise, I covered her body with circular movements, and so long as she seemed indifferent, accepting the procedure without questioning, I continued. After a number of sessions she said, in a semi-inquiring inflection, "That is round?"

"Yes, that is round like a watch and clockwise like the hands of the watch."

After repeating this innumerable times, I changed to "It is also an 'O,' and the letter 'O' is also zero." Then I took her right hand, impelling to it the same circular movement clockwise, still later using her index finger, and finally guiding her index finger over the couch instead of on her body.

I then changed the direction of my movements counterclockwise. This time my answers were, "It is still round. One clockwise, two clockwise, and now one counterclockwise and two counterclockwise. It is zero clockwise, it is still zero counterclockwise. It is the letter 'O' clockwise and again 'O' clockwise, now the same letter 'O' counterclockwise," and so on. I do not know how many dozens or hundreds of repetitions were necessary at each step.

Eventually, I used movements resembling the letter "u" and then alternating "n," letters "w" and "m," and many others. All of them were designed to rebuild awareness of direction and of patterns. I used repetition, contrast, inversion, reversion, and so on to make the building easier. All the complete changes that we use in writing were instilled, rehearsed with constant variations until discrimination occurred. For discrimination occurs or it does not; nobody can make you discriminate. In each instance, the differentiation was noted to have taken place. Differentiation is discrimination with initiative and is the evidence of the successful process of learning. Note the wording I am using. It is important to follow the steps of action instead of thinking in abstract words. Nora's action was passive until something grew in her which bubbled over somehow, one way or another. Then the passivity gradually turned into action, just as the night turns into day with longer or shorter twilights.

Learning is turning darkness, which is the absence of light, into light. Learning is creation. It is making something out of nothing. Learning grows until it dawns on you.

At the end of about three months Nora could hold a pen in a proper writing position, and with my hand reminding her index finger of the movement on the couch of the upward and downward lines and the letter "l" and "i," she managed to reproduce them more or less legibly. Taking abundant time, without jumping to conclusions at every success, we proceeded leisurely with "n," "m," "u," "M," "w," etc. until there was no change in excitation whether I guided her index finger on the table or she scribbled with her pen.

One day she wrote "Nora" about fifty times.

From then until she could sign her name well enough for a legal signature on a check, nothing out of the ordinary happened. Patience, not premeditated but just available, and the gradual transformation of the teacher relationship to person-to-person friendliness, were sufficient to clear the way.

A year later I met Nora strolling on the Bahnhofstrasse in Zurich, just outside the railway station. She had arrived from a small town after an hour-and-a-half train journey. She told me she came to town every Friday to do some shopping from a richer and more elegant selection as well as to visit close friends. Our meeting was that of two friends bumping into each other. A pleasant surprise and no questions asked. The usual commonplace greeting, "Ah, nice to see you," concluded our common/uncommon adventure.

THE ESSENCE

The technical details of my story derive from a working theory I have already described in part.

A working theory cannot be formed without a fundamental relationship to our world. The world around us is our point of view on what life is all about—the *Weltanschauung* of every one of us. In the last resort this is the most important theory of all. Generally, the theory of what life and the cosmos are is ill-founded; essentially unproven beliefs are interwoven into its axioms. Only if and when we know, one day, what the world is about—what life is, what gravitation is, what electricity is, and so on—will a well-founded theory be possible. We already have a considerable body of knowledge about how the world works, but how is very different from what. I know how I live—I do not know what life is. The story I told threw some light on how seeing occurs. I would like you to join me in speculating about other interesting and important issues.

It is highly unlikely that there is any seeing in the darkness of the fetal existence, but there is a sort of hearing. The fetus hears the heartbeats of its mother, the noises of her digestive tract, bubbling of gases of all kinds, sounds of her breathing, coughing, sneezing, and other noises. There is little doubt that noises stimulate the fetus, but we cannot really prove that it hears the way we do. To be stimulated and to respond automatically is very different from hearing after personal growth and experience.

The hearing and the innervation of the ear is thus stimulated in the fetus from the outside, just as it will be when it enters the world. But does the newborn see the outside world when he comes into it? Unlike its ears, its eyes have never been stimulated. It is generally believed that there is no seeing at all before a couple of weeks; there is, however, a sort of response earlier to light. It stands to reason that hearing is prior to seeing in each individual as it is in the evolutionary process in general. Hearing has evolved from responsiveness to mechanical vibrations; responsiveness to finer vibrations, such as oscillations in the air, became hearing when all the structural complexity and finesse of the ear and the nervous system developed. Function and structure grow and assist each other all along the path of evolution.

An infant is predominantly a hearing animal. However, the beginning of his experience of the world around him is first of all sensory, and auditive next. The priority and the order of the two is small and seems to be of no significance at the moment.

The first years of a baby pass in learning to see, to walk, and to speak, and the infant is still largely sensory and auditive. A child's memory, his ability to imitate everything he hears and to learn a second language are significantly greater during the auditive stage than later, when seeing plays a greater role. Many people grow up without ever relating to their

seeing of the outside world: their internal safety is based
more on their hearing; they are sensitive to the inflections of
the voice; the emotional content of the spoken word means
more to them than its meaning. Most of us prefer to hear a
teacher than to learn by reading only, though books are often
more authoritative. Hearing makes seeing more concrete
and easier to remember and therefore also easier to understand. I am referring to our short-term memory without
which it is impossible to relate the end of a sentence to its
beginning.

As the earlier home training of a child in reading and
writing progresses, his hearing attention is gradually with-
drawn from most of the space around him. He learns to
attend increasingly, and often exclusively, to the sector of
space which he sees. We usually see only a small part of our
space, but we hear from all around us.

Here is a particular instance of something very general and
fundamental. The child directing his attention to what his
eyes see withdraws his watchfulness and becomes oblivious
to the greater part of the space around him. Later, he will
learn to listen to the information of both his ears and his eyes.
He already can attend to strong or to optimal stimuli with
both senses, but he will have to learn a lot before he can use
his undivided attention to detect minimal or barely perceptible changes. He will then listen to his ears and check with his
eyes for accuracy and detail.

We have no inkling of the outside world when we arrive
in it. The stimulation of the senses carries no information
except that senses are being stimulated. The beginning of
our acquaintance with the outside world is sensory and entirely subjective, and so for a long time we know only a

sensorial, entirely subjective reality. We are, however, never alone; we are always in communication with other human beings such as parents and teachers. Without ever stopping to think, we behave as if all the others have the same subjective reality. Yet there are as many subjective realities as there are subjects. The part common to all subjective realities is the one objective reality. One objective reality for all—the one we use in communicating with one another.

There is obviously a third Reality, which is more likely older than the other two. This Reality—with a capital R—is understood to exist whether you or I are alive or not, whether we know it or ignore it. It is immensely more complex and only superficially known through science, philosophy, music and poetry.

Our sense of self-importance makes us believe that our subjective reality is as good as all others. Objective reality is that part of our subjective reality which we are willing to concede to our fellowmen. I can see that you see and read; I can never believe that you see as I see, nor read as I do, though I am forced by my own logic to know that I am wrong and that I have no grounds for thinking this. However, my subjective reality is mine entirely and follows all my whims.

Objective reality is less whimsical. It is reality as experienced by all men. It limits and restricts your subjective reality and mine to that on which all the others agree. Subjective reality is anchored in us and is as real as our bodies; objective reality is the measure of our sanity. The Reality has, as yet, never been perceived in its entirety. The belief that we know Reality is an illusion, a Maya, and is a measure of our ignorance.

Mind you, I know that our consciousness and awareness grow. When these are properly understood and developed, we will be able to bite off, chew, and assimilate a much greater chunk of Reality. Our nervous systems are not bound at the start by any reality; *tabulae rasa* they are when we come into the world. On a clean board you can write anything. To make the new writing meaningful and superior to the one we acquired naturally, by chance, this new writing must be based on our choice.

Nora, too, came into the world with a nervous system equipped for all the functions necessary to keep that nervous system growing and learning more and more complex activity. All the digestive and breathing functions, eliminatory mechanisms, regulation of temperature and equilibrium, heartbeat; all the maintenance of invariant pressures of liquids such as blood, lymph and cerebrospinal fluid; everything needed for all the chemical composition; healing and restoring excessive shifts to optimal conditions or homeostasis —all these were there. In short, she had everything any animal has in its nervous system, organized to function and to restore accidental changes of functioning.

But Nora's nervous system, like any other human's, had parts that were not organized at all—only the structure was there with no connections to make it function. This initial state of structure, *tabula rasa*, is capable of functioning only after personal experience of Reality. Reality helps the structure to organize itself to fit the medium in which it will have to live. Entering the world, Nora could not speak any language, walk, read, write, sing, whistle, or yodel. She could not see a three-dimensional object on two-dimensional paper, and she could not count. She had only the structure which could be organized with an astonishing facility to much more than she really did.

She could, in the beginning, have used her nervous system,

the mouth, its muscles, the vocal chords, the feedbacks from the mouth cavity to the ears and auditory cortex to fit any of two thousand languages, and at least as many dialects, with equal facility.

The human species started as an animal which turned out to be Homo sapiens. All other animals come into the world with their structures much more organized to function in almost rigid patterns. Their nervous systems are more complete and the patterns of connections directing activity are almost set and unalterable, but fit for early action. Homo sapiens arrives with a tremendous part of his nervous mass left unpatterned, unconnected, so that each individual, depending on where he happens to be born, can organize his brain to fit the demands of his surrounding. This his brain learns to do. The animal part, which is ready at birth, can only do what other animals do. Man's brain can learn to do in many ways what other animals can do only in one fixed way.

The freedom to learn is a great liability, and a restriction from the start. There is no freedom of choice or free will where there is only one way of acting. Learning makes it possible to choose among alternative ways of acting. The ability to learn is synonymous with free choice and free will. But once learned, the choice is made, the die is cast, and the *tabula rasa* is no more. Herein lie the liabilities as well as the restrictions.

As the awareness of being Homo sapiens evolved, very slowly his ways of learning grew, gradually and naturally. There was no thought-out method of education. Methods which came naturally when dealing with an infant continued, essentially the same, forever after. At the age of two, when our nervous system attains four-fifths of its ultimate size and weight, everything is set and learning will continue on the preset lines, restricting the freedom of learning and choice in most cases.

Nora, like every one of us, was not aware that the functions she had lost were originally learned and not inherited as was her digestion or temperature regulation. Were these latter lost, then life would come to an end, but she had lost learned organization and like everybody else saw no difference between the Homo sapiens part of her and the animal part. She could not help herself and neither could anybody who was not aware of the difference. Many of the evils from which we suffer are rooted in our conception of human education as the training of a complete being to do this or that, as though we were making a computer perform a desired activity.

In spite of the apparent doom of the human future, I believe we have not yet reached Homo sapiens' capacity for learning. It is too early to condemn man on the strength of the little awareness he has acquired by chance and not by his outstanding ability to reduce greater complexity to familiar simplicity—in other words, to learn. We have never yet used our essential freedom of choice and we have barely learned to learn.

It is difficult to choose a suitable example to illustrate the above, but here is a simple one, showing that our ignorant learning is both a liability and a restriction. Blindfold yourself in your house, in familiar surroundings, and live by yourself for half an hour to begin with. You will realize that your awareness is always limited, mostly to what you can see. Anyone who must himself ensure his individual safety and security could not survive with two-thirds of the space around him neglected and below his level of awareness. When we attend to what we see, we withdraw attention from the greater part of space. A wild animal that has not the awareness of a samurai, knowing what happens behind it and above, cannot last very long. You and I can do what a trained samurai can do. We can restrain and extend our awareness to the objective reality all around ourselves. Our ears did so before their information began to be partially ignored or neglected, before our vision became domineering instead of dominant.

If you continue the exercise and rely on your ears exclusively until you can manage for a couple of hours without injuring yourself, you will realize how poorly we use ourselves even when our eyes are open. You will experience not only wider attention, but the tonus of your entire being will be heightened to buoyancy and freshness of both subjective and objective reality. Some esoteric disciplines believe that the entire consciousness is raised to a higher level. Obviously, your memory will resemble what it was in your childhood before you learned to read. Your ability to learn and retain will improve. Older people learn poorly, essentially because they attend with only a small part of their awareness. What they learn is not associated with their entire beings as it is in childhood. It is the difference between trying to learn the telephone number of a casual acquaintance and that of someone you love.

QUESTIONS—
AND AVOIDING
ANSWERING THEM
FULLY

Now that you have read about this adventure in the mysterious brain jungle of familiar everyday acts, you will certainly have found more than one query or objection to my tale. I promised you that I would answer questions, but more concisely than in my story. So here I am—please shoot!

Q. *At one instant you said something like: "I saw that the trouble must be somewhere higher in the brain." What do you mean by "higher" in the brain?*

A. John Hughlings Jackson's law says: The nerve functions which are the latest to develop are the earliest to be destroyed. This is correct when applied to every individual as well as to the species as a whole. Thus, if a person is knocked unconscious in an accident he will forget the last minutes before the accident and will be unable to tell the circumstances of the happening. If the trauma is severe, he may forget the last years before it, but recall his earlier past. Sometimes he may forget all the languages he knew except his mother tongue. Jackson maintained that the earlier a brain function occurred in evolution, the lower it is when considering the entire nervous system being held vertical, as in standing. The spinal cord developed earlier than the higher parts. The thalamus, which is the seat of the emotions, developed earlier than the forebrain. This is to illustrate the principle.

Each new development which lies actually on the old structure may put a brake on the lower function. The lower function is then more evenly performed, more graded. The lower elementary conduction in nerves or contraction in muscular fibers is of the all-or-none kind. Gradation of activity is obtained through higher centers. Upper layers may also excite lower structures. A clot in the brain may produce a spastic paralysis or a flaccid one, depending on the "height" of the clot. In the first case an inhibiting layer has been destroyed; in the second, an excitatory one has been damaged.

Not very many decades ago brain physiology often consisted in finding which slice had to be cut, starting from the top, to induce a change in the behavior of the animal. This was called a preparation. Thus, in slicing off layer after layer until the red nucleus was sliced off, say in a cat, first the legs became suddenly stronger, then the cat had limp toneless paws. When most of the brain was cut off, there appeared decerebrated rigidity, when the legs straightened with astonishing power, so much so that it became practically impossible to bend a paw without damaging it.

It is in this sense that the expressions "higher centers" and "lower centers" were used. But please do not ask now where the red nucleus is. Look it up in an atlas of the brain or book of anatomy. You may also know what it does, but you will have to work a little harder for that.

Q. *You stressed the difference between Nora's recovering her writing ability and recreating the same ability. How can you recreate an ability?*

A. An ability results from a structure being trained until a skilled functioning is obtained. The ability is erratic and rudimentary in the beginning. In due time and with sufficient variations the ability becomes a skill. During that time a large number of cells in the nervous system have been involved. When a skill cannot be performed as before, only some of the cells which were essential to the skillful performance do not function. There might be a multitude of cells that were auxiliary to the skill. In some cases it is possible to complete the differentiation of the auxiliary parts to perform the skill, though usually in a different manner. This is recreating something and not restoring it to what it was before.

Q. *You said it was important to estimate the age to which the function has regressed in planning recovery. Please comment.*

A. If somebody is unconscious, there is no point in speaking to him. He has regressed to an age long prior to speech. It is useless to try to teach dancing to a man who cannot crawl on all fours. He must be first taught to crawl, to walk, to run before being taught to dance. This crudely answers your question.

Q. *What do you mean by saying "try not to think in words"?*

A. If you are told that somebody cannot do something, logically there is nothing you can do about it. Every diagnosis in words inhibits the brain from thinking for itself. If words say "incurable" the situation will not be changed by saying "curable." But if you use your sensory ability to look, learn, listen, and touch you may find new data which will make you see what you can do to help.

Q. *Your reference to abstractions is generally derogatory: please comment.*

A. Most nouns are symbols. "Chair" is a symbol, as it identifies none of the several hundred different pieces of furniture on which one person may sit, and it is also an abstraction, as there is nothing concrete about the concept "chair." There is nothing wrong with abstractions so long as we agree that words are primarily or exclusively for communication.

When words like "orientation" and "unconscious" were formulated they were used to sum up, or shorten, a detailed description of a concept. Over time, however, with increased familiarity the word tends to become a thing—a something which exists. The word "unconscious" has long ceased to describe a complex and has become a thing. When you think or say something, who does it? You or your unconscious? There is no simple answer. A long clarification of the different levels of the abstractions "you" and "unconscious" is necessary.

Everyone uses abstractions, but one is at a loss to know what to do when "equilibrium" or "orientation" go wrong. What does one do to restore equilibrium in a person suffering from ataxia? Equilibrium does not exist nor is it lacking in ataxia. In such a case the details of ataxia and of equilibrium from which these abstractions were derived in the first place are more useful for being more concrete. In short, abstractions make thinking sluggish and disoriented.

Q. *Would you clarify orientation as related to body aware-ness?*

A. I am glad you asked this question as it can illustrate admirably my reply to the previous one. Both words are abstractions, and so long as I do not think of the activities from which they were abstracted—and for which they now stand—there is nothing to tell me which is the more general term. A tree orients itself, every living thing orients itself, and man orients himself. None need awareness to do so.

Body awareness enables us to know we orient ourselves. In man the complexity is even greater. For an infant orients himself as an animal does, but a man knows how to get "there" and in "time."

Q. *Do you view all abstractions with the same attitude as those relating to human affairs?*

A. Yes. Take for instance "velocity." Can you increase or decrease a velocity? No one can do anything with abstractions such as velocity orientation or whatever. One has to know the velocity of what is to be changed. One can change the velocity of one's bicycle, car, and so on, but one cannot change the velocity of light, or accelerate the earth or the sun. Similarly, one cannot change the notion orientation unless one knows whose orientation and what precise defect one deals with. The semicircular canals may be defective. A variety of feedbacks to the nervous system may be defective and so much else may be wrong. The familiar words lull us often into complacency and in such cases hinder constructive thinking.